ALL ABOUT DINOSAURS

IGUANODON

by

Mignonne Gunasekara

BookLife
PUBLISHING

©2020
BookLife Publishing Ltd.
King's Lynn
Norfolk PE30 4LS

A catalogue record for this book is available from the British Library.

ISBN: 978-1-83927-065-9

Written by:
Mignonne Gunasekara

Edited by:
Shalini Vallepur

Designed by:
Amy Li

PHOTO CREDITS

CONTENTS

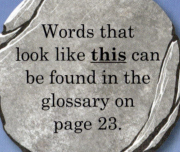

Words that look like **this** can be found in the glossary on page 23.

WHAT WERE DINOSAURS?

Dinosaurs were **<u>reptiles</u>** that lived on Earth for over 160 million years before they went **<u>extinct</u>**.

There were many different types of gigantic reptile. They lived both on land and in water – and some could even fly!

WHEN WERE DINOSAURS ALIVE?

Dinosaurs first lived around 245 million years ago during a period of time called the **Mesozoic Era**. The last dinosaurs went extinct around 66 million years ago, long before the first humans were ever alive.

Millions of years ago, all the land on Earth was together in one piece. But during the time of the dinosaurs, it slowly broke up into the different **continents** that we know today.

PANGEA

WHEN ALL THE LAND ON EARTH WAS TOGETHER IN ONE PIECE, IT WAS CALLED PANGEA.

HOW DO WE KNOW...?

We know so much about dinosaurs thanks to the scientists, called palaeontologists (pay-lee-on-tol-uh-gists), who study them. They dig up **fossils** of dinosaurs to find out more about them.

Ammonite FOSSILS

FOSSILISED DINOSAUR EGGS

Palaeontologists put together the bones they find to try to make full dinosaur skeletons. From these skeletons, palaeontologists can often work out the size and weight of a dinosaur. They can also find out information about what it ate from nearby fossils and fossilised poo.

PALAEONTOLOGISTS HAVE EVEN FOUND FOSSILISED EGGS AND FOOTPRINTS BELONGING TO DINOSAURS.

DINOSAUR FOOTPRINT

IGUANODON SKULL

IGUANODON

Mary and Gideon Mantell found the first signs of Iguanodon in England. They found teeth in rocks. They knew from the size and shape of the teeth that this dinosaur was a large **herbivore**.

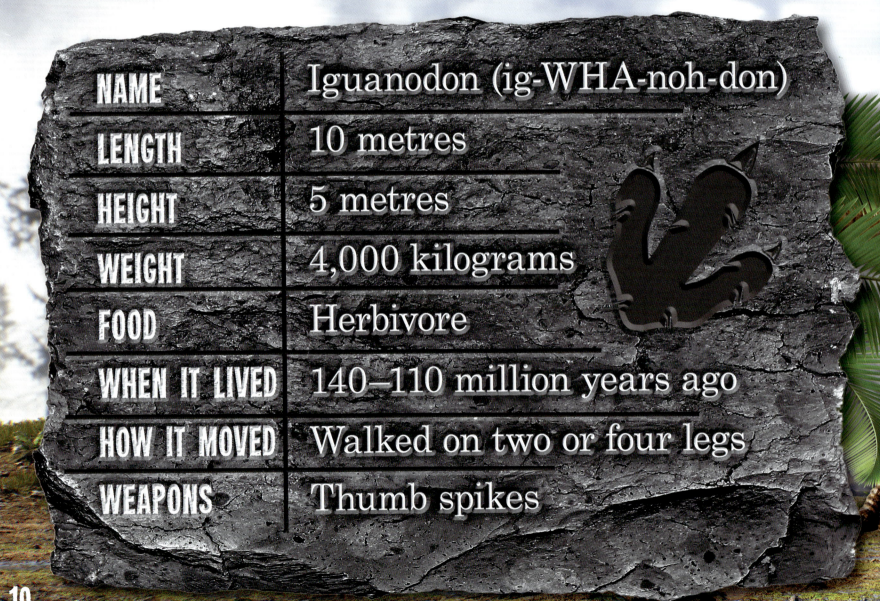

NAME	Iguanodon (ig-WHA-noh-don)
LENGTH	10 metres
HEIGHT	5 metres
WEIGHT	4,000 kilograms
FOOD	Herbivore
WHEN IT LIVED	140–110 million years ago
HOW IT MOVED	Walked on two or four legs
WEAPONS	Thumb spikes

Gideon Mantell named the **discovery** 'Iguanodon' because its teeth reminded him of a modern-day iguana's teeth, but much bigger. Iguanodon was the first herbivorous dinosaur to be discovered and the second dinosaur to ever be discovered.

THE NAME 'IGUANODON' MEANS 'IGUANA TOOTH'.

IGUANODON

BARYONYX

WHAT DID IGUANODON LOOK LIKE?

Iguanodon had a beak that was probably covered in keratin. This is the same thing your hair and fingernails are made of. Iguanodon is most famous for the special cone-shaped spikes it had as thumbs.

THUMB SPIKE

IGUANODON WOULD HAVE SPENT MORE TIME ON TWO LEGS WHEN IT WAS YOUNG BECAUSE ITS ARMS WOULD HAVE BEEN SHORTER.

Iguanodon had to stand on all fours as it got older because parts of its **spine** would join together. This led to a stiff tail that stuck out straight behind Iguanodon.

IGUANODON WAS LARGE AND BULKY WITH A STIFF TAIL.

WHERE DID IGUANODON LIVE?

Iguanodon lived during the **Early Cretaceous Period**. Iguanodon fossils have been found in Belgium, the US and England. Palaeontologists think Iguanodon probably lived in other European countries too, as similar dinosaurs were found in Spain.

THE UK

WEST SUSSEX   MAIDSTONE

ISLE OF WIGHT   BERNISSART

BELGIUM

THE UK

BELGIUM

SOUTH DAKOTA

THE US

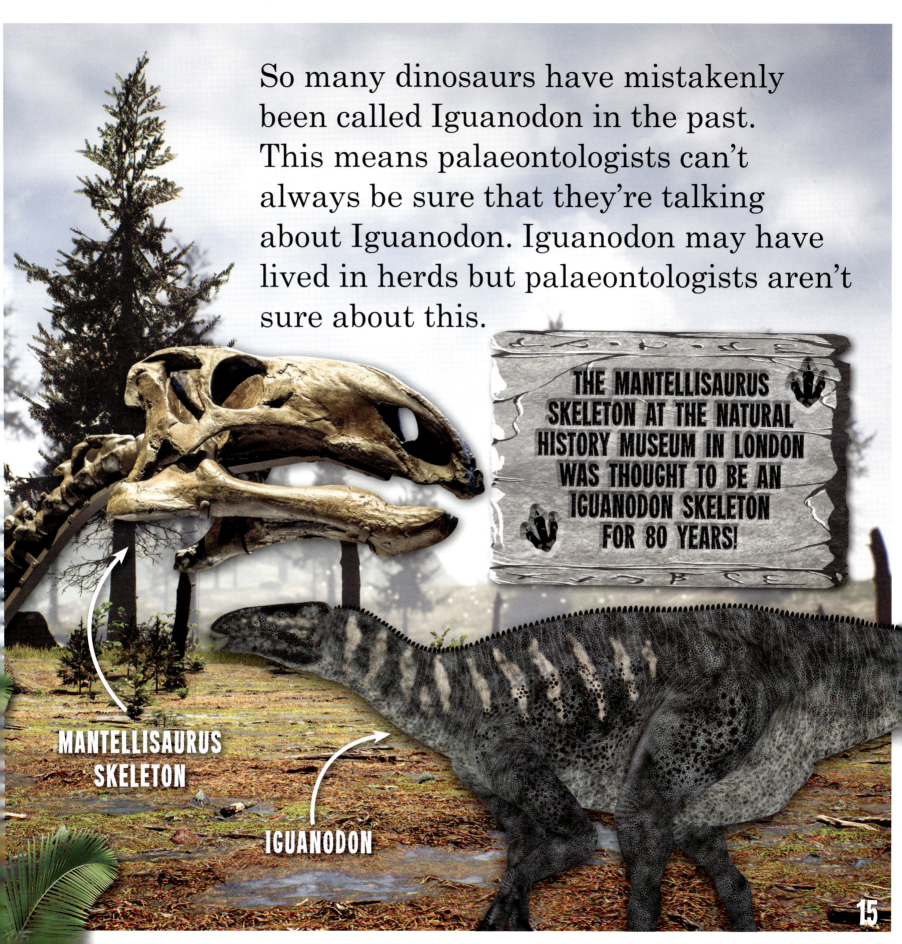

So many dinosaurs have mistakenly been called Iguanodon in the past. This means palaeontologists can't always be sure that they're talking about Iguanodon. Iguanodon may have lived in herds but palaeontologists aren't sure about this.

THE MANTELLISAURUS SKELETON AT THE NATURAL HISTORY MUSEUM IN LONDON WAS THOUGHT TO BE AN IGUANODON SKELETON FOR 80 YEARS!

MANTELLISAURUS SKELETON

IGUANODON

WHAT DID IGUANODON EAT?

Iguanodon had a beak instead of front teeth, which would have been used to bite off plants to chew. Its teeth were the perfect shape to grind up tough plants.

EARLY DRAWING OF AN IGUANODON TOOTH

TOOTHLESS BEAK

IGUANODON'S TEETH WOULD HAVE BEEN REPLACED BY NEW ONES WHEN THEY BECAME TOO WORN OUT.

Iguanodon probably ate plants such as ferns, which grew low on the ground near rivers and streams. Iguanodon fossils make palaeontologists think it had some kind of cheek pouch to hold food in its mouth.

DID IGUANODON HAVE THE SPIKIEST THUMB?

Palaeontologists aren't sure what Iguanodon used its thumb spike for. It might have been a weapon for defending itself against **predators** or other similar dinosaurs, or to help Iguanodon eat by breaking into seeds and fruits.

IGUANODON THUMB SPIKE

UTAHRAPTOR
CLAW

Utahraptor, the biggest of all **raptors**, had a claw on each foot that was probably around 38 centimetres long! It would have used this claw to slash at its **prey**... which would have included Iguanodon.

FACTS ABOUT
IGUANODON

When Mantell first tried to show what Iguanodon looked like, he put its thumb spike as a horn on its nose instead! Maybe he was thinking of the rhinoceros iguana's horn when he did this.

RHINOCEROS IGUANA

AN OLD, INCORRECT IDEA OF WHAT IGUANODON LOOKED LIKE

RHINOCEROS IGUANA'S HORN

People used to think that Iguanodon stood like a kangaroo, but palaeontologists now believe it probably switched between walking on four legs or two legs most of the time, then used two legs while running.

IGUANODON WOULD HAVE HAD TO HAVE ITS TAIL BROKEN FOR IT TO STAND LIKE THIS.

BEAK

THUMB SPIKE

STIFF TAIL

THREE TOES

IGUANO-DON'T-YOU-SEE?

Can you find the five differences between these two scenes?

The answers can be found on page 24.

GLOSSARY

ammonite	a type of sea creature with flat, spiral shells that no longer exists
continents	large areas of land that are made up of many countries
discovery	something that has been found, especially for the first time
Early Cretaceous Period	the period of time between 145 and 100.5 million years ago
extinct	no longer existing
fossils	parts and traces of plants and animals from a long time ago that have been kept in good condition inside rocks
herbivore	an animal that only eats plants
Mesozoic Era	the period of time between 250 and 66 million years ago, when dinosaurs lived
predators	animals that hunt other animals for food
prey	animals that are hunted by other animals for food
raptors	meat-eating dinosaurs belonging to a group that includes Velociraptor and Utahraptor
reptiles	cold-blooded animals that are usually covered in scales
spine	the set of bones that make up the back

INDEX